Small Lives

Photographs of Irish Childhood

1860–1970

Edited by Aoife O'Connor

Gill & Macmillan
Hume Avenue, Park West, Dublin 12
with associated companies throughout the world
www.gillmacmillanbooks.ie

© Text, Aoife O'Connor 2012
© Images, National Library of Ireland 2012
978 07171 5462 3

Design and print origination by Design Image
Printed in Poland

This book is typeset in 11 pt Portland LDO on 16 pt leading.

1 3 5 4 2

Contents

Acknowledgments

I gratefully acknowledge all of the assistance I received in putting together the original 'Small Lives' exhibition for the National Library of Ireland and this book. Without the knowledge of the staff at the NLI I might have missed some of the most striking images contained here: Andrea Bonnie, Ben Crane, Elizabeth Kirwan, Carol Maddock, Riona McMorrow, Katherine McSharry, Keith Murphy, Bríd O'Sullivan, Fiona Ross, Sara Smyth, Noel Stapleton.

And to the staff at Gill & Macmillan who supported the project and guided me through the whole process: Fergal Tobin, Ciara O'Connor, Deirdre Rennison Kunz.

I would also like to thank my friend Eimear Ging for her suggestions, and to my husband, Frank O'Gorman, for his unfailing and continued support, my love.

Introduction

Childhood is a universal experience. We were all children once. However, as will be seen from the diversity of the photographs in this book, there is no typical childhood.

Many of the children in the photographs contained here are anonymous. The familiarity of family, the fleeting moment of a good 'shot' or the business of running a photographic studio all contribute to this anonymity. Anonymity can be beneficial. It frees us to imagine the lives of these children beyond the photographs, and allows them to represent their time and place, without the encumbrance of their specific stories. The photographs depict a variety of childhood experiences across the decades and the social classes, in urban and rural settings. Seeing our past and our culture through the children in these photographs, we can more easily inhabit the scenes they portray. Remembering our childhood selves, we can imagine what our reactions and feelings might have been had we lived in their time, experienced their lives. Anonymity can also tantalise and frustrate. In many instances we are left wondering who these children were and how their lives turned out. Their photographs are all we have left to record their existence.

Photography frames and freezes a point in time. The choices made by a photographer at that moment determine how it will be seen and understood by future generations. Photography both records events and, in their recording, creates events. The very act of photographing something makes it special, even extraordinary. The portrayal of childhood in these photographs is mediated in part by the historical limitations of photography and by the interests of the individual photographers whose work has been acquired by the NLI. In deciding which images to include, those that featured children alone were favoured over those showing a mix of children and adults. The children are all, as far as could be discerned, under the age of sixteen. The formality of dress before the 1950s can make many of the children look older than their years. Others are engaged in work no longer considered suitable for children. Perhaps they did not even see themselves as children.

In the early days of photography the technology, in common with most new technologies, was available only to those who could afford it: both financially, and in terms of leisure time. Early cameras were expensive and cumbersome and required the photographer to have access to their own darkroom for processing negatives. In the 1860s owning a camera was the preserve of dedicated, well-off amateurs, and professional studios. The images from those earlier decades are formal and are similar, in many respects, to painted portraits. Long exposure times and contemporary mores led to sitters having serious, if not seemingly sullen, expressions. As in art portraiture, studios employed practical and symbolic props — a chair to sit or lean on made posing more comfortable; a potted plant, toy or swing added depth and interest. Backdrops also changed over the decades, from neutral to elaborate and back to neutral again.

Over the ensuing decades experimentation led to innovation, and cheaper and more user-friendly cameras were produced. By the 1890s cameras with pre-loaded film, producing black and white images, were being sold to a mass-market audience. Although studio portraiture remained popular, these portable cameras led to greater variety and a degree of spontaneity in photography. This is reflected in the images in the volume dating to that period. Photography could now also be used to document events, and the images used to draw attention to particular causes with new immediacy and force. Pictures of the disadvantaged and destitute could be used to elicit sympathies and funds as well as to engender change. Colour photography was the next innovation. It accompanied ever cheaper, easier to use and more sophisticated cameras. In particular these cameras were better able to compensate for movement, which previously caused indistinct and blurred images, a perennial problem when photographing restless children, who often also delight in challenging a photographer. As cameras improved, amateur photographers abounded, and colour, which mirrored reality, became the norm, the 'mood' of the photographs also changed. The quest for natural expression and experiments with framing moved the medium away from the formality of the earlier decades; a touch of chaos (so natural to children) becomes apparent in the images from the later decades. In these images the children balance on walls, jostle each other for position and strike whatever pose takes their fancy. They can regard or disregard the photographer; they are under no obligation to follow his instruction. He is not the novelty he once was, his camera no longer an object of intrigue or wonder. He no longer controls how they are portrayed, although the camera still has an effect on their behaviour.

As a record of the variety of childhood experiences possible over a century this volume does not seek to define the parameters of childhood, neither does it claim to be a comprehensive portrait of the experience of an 'Irish childhood', if such a thing can even be said to exist. Instead it offers a visual record which it is hoped will complement the work of historians and appeal to all.

Note: The lack of dates on many of the photographs provided its own challenges. In these instances the internal evidence of the photograph (clothes and studio dressing) as well as the format of the original (glass plate, *carte de visite*) helped with dating. Very occasionally, other objects in the photograph narrowed the date, e.g. a poster. Dates have been given as a single year but, where the exact date is unknown, a margin of error of ±5 years is likely.

METAL MAN. TRAMORE. Co. WATERFORD. 9054. W.L.

Photographs of Irish Childhood 1860–1970

1866 | Co. Louth/India

Breeching. Matthew Charles Edward Fortescue aged five. The velvet suit is in a style popular for newly breeched boys, i.e., those wearing trousers for the first time. Even among the well-off, portraits were generally reserved for special occasions and milestones, such as breeching. The bolero jacket Matthew is wearing is designed to be fastened at the throat and the loose knee-length breeches are less restrictive than adult trousers. Matthew's father served as a major in the British army in India, where he had a second family. He died of cholera in India the year after this photograph of his son was taken.

Album 97

1

1875

Stephenstown, Co. Louth

Woollen Suit. Matthew now aged fourteen, dressed in more sober attire. Matthew became High Sheriff of Louth in 1903 and held the rank of major in the 6th Battalion of the Royal Irish Rifles.

Album 97

J·GALBRAITH   DU·NDALK

c. 1867

Santry, Dublin

Miss Domville. Mary Adelaide Domville at about twelve years of age. She wears a typical mid-1860s dress, supported underneath by a crinoline hoop. Around her neck is a ribbon choker decorated with bells. Fashions for older children were often miniature versions of adult clothes. The Domvilles held the baronetcy of Santry and lived at Santry Court, Dublin. The house was built in 1708, but was sadly destroyed by fire in 1948, and demolished in 1959.

Album 426

3

c. 1868 | Santry, Dublin

Beatrice. Early photographic portraiture replicated, in some respects, the symbolism of art. Beatrice is shown with her hand on a book, indicating she is educated and literate. The pedestal, visible at her feet, provides something to lean against to help steady her for the long exposure required by early cameras. Smiling was discouraged as it is a difficult expression to maintain with any degree of naturalness for long periods of time, and portraits were intended to convey the dignity of the subject.

Album 426

ANCIENT CROSS, CONG. CO. GALWAY. 1122. W.L.

1869 | Cong, Co. Mayo

Market Cross, Cong. This solitary boy sits on the plinth of the Market Cross in Cong. His well-worn and torn trousers are made from corduroy, a practical fabric associated with labourers in the nineteenth century. The inscription on the cross, now faded, is written in old Irish and asks the viewer to pray for previous abbots of the monastery. Pasted to the pillar is an advertisement for a three-day train excursion to Dublin for passengers of the *Eglinton* pleasure cruiser. The *Eglinton*, a steamer, was purpose built in 1862 for tourist cruises of Lough Corrib.

Lawrence Collection

5

c. 1873 | Galway

Baron in Waiting. Robert Edward Dillon surrounded by his toys, aged four. His outfit indicates he is yet to be breeched; he may have had to wait until being sent to school, at around age seven, to get his first pair of trousers. His open-fronted jacket is in the *zouave* style which was popular from the 1860s. As Luke Dillon's only son, Robert inherited the family title and became the fifth and last Baron of Clonbrock.

Clonbrock Collection

1 July 1873 | Galway

Posing with Dolly. Georgiana Dillon standing on the sweeping steps of Clonbrock House, two months after her sixth birthday. The impressive estate was broken up and sold off over the years and the family's income was greatly reduced during the economic depression of the 1920s and 1930s. The house was destroyed by a fire in 1994. Georgiana does not appear to have ever married; she was still living at Clonbrock House in 1901 at the age of thirty-three and died in 1942.

Clonbrock Collection

1879

Westmeath

Mary Cassandra. The little girl staring out from this photograph with her solemn face is something of a mystery. Although her name and the date of the photograph give us more information than we have for many of the other children in the collection, very little is known about her. A glimpse of her petticoat can be seen as she perches precariously on the overstuffed chair. Her dress, styled on adult clothing, is shortened as a concession to her young age, five years old.

Album 200

JAMES MAGILL   BELFAST

c. 1883 | Stephenstown, Co. Louth

Agnes. Dressed in elbow-length lace gloves and an elaborately flounced dress, Agnes is on the cutting edge of 1880s fashion and looks rather older than her three years. She appears resigned to her elaborate, and no doubt costly, outfit. During the nineteenth and early twentieth centuries, even very young children were accustomed to wearing hats and other cumbersome accessories, such as Agnes's lace fichu worn crossed over her torso. Photographic studios also changed according to fashions and in the 1880s naturalistic backdrops and accessories, such as the rocks and ferns seen here, were favoured.

Album 98

9

Sep. 22/83 XIX

22 September 1883

Galway

Edith and Ethel. Edith and Ethel Dillon, daughters of the fourth Baron Clonbrock in County Galway, grew up in a world of privilege, surrounded by butlers, footmen and lady's-maids. The 1901 census return shows eleven house-servants, and fifty tenants and other servants on the estate. There were just six people in the immediate family. Edith (*on the right*) was born in 1878 and married in January 1905 at the age of 26. Ethel (*on the left*) was born in 1880, did not marry and lived at the estate until the 1960s.

Clonbrock Collection

c. 1885 | Galway

Alphabet Blocks. Sisters Edith and Ethel Dillon play with *Young England's Floral Alphabet* blocks. They are playing outside the family's specially built photographic darkroom. The family were keen photographers and their substantial collection of over three thousand images, housed in the NLI, documents family and estate life from the 1860s to the 1930s.

Clonbrock Collection

c. 1886

Westmeath

Pantalettes. Wearing a home-made navy summer dress and pantalettes trimmed in eyelet lace, the little girl poses in a studio decorated in a style typical of the 1880s, with an outdoor theme. Pantalettes, trouser-like underwear, were going out of fashion in the 1880s. Previously they would have been worn by both boys and girls, and were nearly always visible below their frocks, preserving the modesty of the wearer.

Album 200

1887 | Wexford

Eviction. The precarious life of a tenant farmer must have been keenly felt by parents, whose young children could find themselves sleeping in a roughly made sod house or under a hedge should the family be evicted. This photograph is part of the Coolgreany Album which documents the eviction of several families from the Coolgreany estate in County Wexford in 1887. Eviction was not reserved for those who could not pay their rent; it was often used as a means to clear land of small farmers to make way for more efficient and profitable land management practices.

Coolgreany Evictions Album

c. 1888 | Glenbeigh, Co. Kerry

Eviction Huts. Huts like this one in Glenbeigh were usually built as temporary, seasonal shelters by shepherds and herders. Made of dry-stone walling and sod, and measuring just six feet by five feet, and four and a half feet in height, this hut was shelter to a family of ten after their eviction. Further misery could be visited upon the family as these dwellings could be deemed unhygienic by local authorities and torn down, leaving a family with nowhere to go.

Eblana Collection

c. 1887

Fermoy, Co. Cork

Welch Fusiliers. Based in Fermoy from 1887, the Royal Welch Fusiliers have kept a goat as their mascot since 1777. Since 1844 they have received their goat from the royal Cashmere (Kashmir) herd. As in many regiments, the care of the mascot fell to a drummer boy, pictured here in parade dress.

Lawrence Collection

c. 1887 | Tramore, Co. Waterford

Summer House. Young Master White sports a sporran almost as big as himself! His younger brother or sister escapes wearing traditional costume.

A.H. Poole Collection

KEEL VILLAGE. ACHILL . 5092 .W L .

c. 1888 | Achill Island, Co. Mayo

Keel Village. The advances in photographic technology in the 1880s meant that photographers could more easily take their craft to potential subjects and document the world around them. It is probable that this image was taken soon after the opening of the bridge from Achill to the mainland made the island more accessible.

Lawrence Collection

19

c. 1888 | Waterford

Holiday Home. One of several images of the Tobin family in the NLI's collection, which appear to have been taken on the same day at various locations around what may have been their holiday home in Tramore. The children's white outfits, complete with silk sashes and Tam-o'-Shanter inspired hats, don't seem particularly suited to play.

A.H. Poole Collection

c. 1890 | Waterford

Pigs in the Parlour. Having their photograph taken was likely a novel experience for this family. Some have decked themselves out in their best, donning hats and shoes, although others appear to have been prevailed upon while they sat knitting in the sunshine. The inclusion of the pigs, who were probably enticed to stay in shot by giving them something to eat, seems a deliberate decision by the photographer to portray an unsophisticated, rustic view of cottage life.

A.H. Poole Collection

21

THE BRIDGE. INCHIGEELA. Co. CORK. 8782. W.L.

c. 1890

Inchigeela, Co. Cork

At Work or at Play? These children might be working or playing in this wheat field on the banks of the River Lee at Inchigeela. During the nineteenth century, children often missed school in order to work in industry, in family businesses or on the family farm. Compulsory schooling for all children between the ages of six and fourteen was law by 1898. However, exceptions were made. In 1926 the revised Education Act allowed for children to be removed from school for ten days between March and May, and again, for another ten days, between August and October, to help on the family farm.

Lawrence Collection

c. 1892

Connemara

Froebel's First Gift. Pictured outside their school in Connemara, Co. Galway, these children are being shown Froebel's 'first gift', a sphere on a string. Froebel's gifts are coloured shapes designed to teach children through touch and play. The introduction of new teaching methods was very much in keeping with the 'improving' ethos of James Hack Tuke, an English philanthropist who took a particular, and lifelong, interest in alleviating the poverty he saw in the west of Ireland after an 1847 visit. Images such as this could be used in slideshows to show subscribers where their funds were being used and to raise further funds for Tuke's philanthropic work in the west of Ireland.

Tuke Collection

c. 1892 | Connemara

Schoolgirls. According to the photographer, the children did not recognise themselves in the photograph, although they could point out their friends. The photographer attributes this to their never having seen their own reflections. 'A remarkable fact with reference to the school groups is that the children on being shown the photograph, as an object lesson, know each other at once but not one recognises himself or herself (never having seen that same — looking glasses being unknown).'

Tuke Collection

c. 1892 | Connemara

Schoolboys. Although it was quite normal in the late nineteenth and early twentieth centuries to dress young boys and girls the same way, in tunics or dresses, it is a little surprising to see boys who appear to be as old as twelve being dressed in this way. Folk beliefs regarding fairies stealing boys rather than girls may have contributed to the custom of dressing boys as 'girls'. Only two of the boys boast trousers, probably handed down from older brothers. Despite their lack of trousers, most of the boys' waistcoats and jackets are fully buttoned up and most have hats. Writing in *Irish Distress and its Remedies* Tuke notes, 'Some of the children were very poorly clad, and we were told that the want of clothing prevented the attendance [at school] of many.'

Tuke Collection

c. 1895

Waterford

Stable-boy. The towering horse does not appear to fluster this barefoot stable-boy. It is possible that he did not think of himself as a child. Working conferred new status as a wage earner on a young boy or girl which could often be a matter of pride, elevating them beyond the position of mere 'child'. Many children worked and attended school, often in the evenings after what would now be considered a full day's work.

A.H. Poole Collection

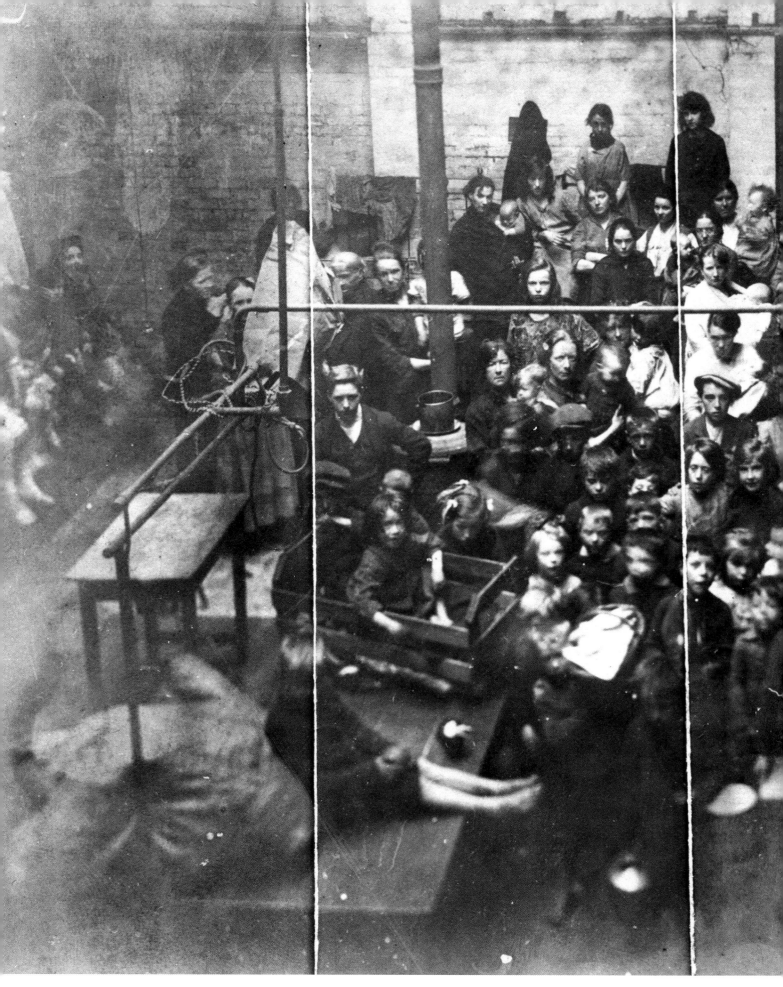

c. 1895

Dublin

The Workhouse. Workhouses were catch-all places for those unable to support themselves, the abandoned, the destitute, the sick, the elderly, and those with intellectual disabilities. Overcrowding and unsanitary conditions were perennial problems. It was usual to separate the men from the women and children, and often children were separated from both parents.

Irish Personalities List

c. 1895 | Waterford

Family. We do not know the name of this large family. Given the similarities in boys' and girls' clothes at the time, it is not possible to tell if the three younger children are boys or girls. The child on the father's lap has white socks, whereas the rest have black; perhaps this indicates a girl? They are, at the very least, dressed in their best. The photograph appears to have been taken to celebrate the youngest child's christening.

A.H. Poole Collection

BOTANIC GARDENS. BELFAST. 2380. W.L.

c. 1895 | Belfast

Botanic Gardens, Belfast. The Botanic Gardens opened to the public in 1895. The Palm House in the background is a fine example of Victorian architecture. The children seem to be alone but it is more likely that their parents and nannies are hidden behind the photographer. The long shadows cast by the children would indicate that the photograph was taken in either early morning or late evening. This suggests the children were brought to the gardens especially to be photographed, and may explain the lack of other visitors to the gardens.

Lawrence Collection

c. 1897

Unknown

Paddling. Modesty was extremely important in the late nineteenth century, even at the seaside, and it would have been almost unthinkable for these girls to go swimming. The girls have made the best of the situation and, with their hats still on, they have tucked up their long skirts, revealing their bloomers, to paddle in the sea. As they hold onto each other they seem to be daring each other to go deeper into the waves.

Clarke Collection

c. 1897 | Bray, Co. Wicklow

What's out there? Something has caught the children's attention while paddling at the beach: a passing sailboat perhaps? Or perhaps a bathing machine being rolled out to deeper water?

Clarke Collection

c. 1897 | Bray, Co. Wicklow

Bathing Machine. The two children are seated on the back of a bathing machine. These horse-drawn changing rooms allowed women, in particular, to enter and exit the sea without being seen. Bathing was promoted for its health benefits rather than as a recreation. Bathers would immerse themselves for a few minutes before returning to the bathing box, which would then be rolled back to shore. Modesty was further protected by having separate bathing areas for men, women and children.

Clarke Collection

c. 1897

Unknown

Cycling along the Promenade. The exuberance of the young girl cycling along the promenade is a carefree celebration of childhood. The tricycle, which became popular in the 1870s, was considered more suitable for 'young ladies'. As she careens along the seafront, this girl is obviously not interested in being 'ladylike'. In the background we can see a young boy swinging his spade as he walks ahead of his mother or nanny. Seaside resorts became more accessible in the nineteenth century thanks to the development of the railways.

Clarke Collection

39

WORK ROOM. BALTIMORE SCHOOL. 2594 W. L.

c. 1897 Baltimore, Co. Cork

Baltimore Fisheries School. Established in 1887, the
Baltimore Industrial School accommodated over
150 boys under the age of sixteen. In its early years
the school taught useful trades such as net-
making and ship-building, but conditions were
harsh and in later years abuse was rife. The boys
are dressed in a simple uniform and their hair is
kept short, perhaps to make it easier to check for
lice. The school was finally closed in 1950.

Lawrence Collection

BALTIMORE SCHOOL . 5193 . W.L .

c. 1897 | Baltimore, Co. Cork

Net Making. The net-making workshop of the Fisheries School in Baltimore. Each year the board's report appeared in the local paper and listed where the boys had been placed after leaving the school, 'when their detention under the Industrial Schools Act was no longer possible … in Trades or businesses, 7; in farming, labouring, & c, 8; in the army, 2; in the navy, 2; in seafaring, 2; in fishing, 1; emigrated, 1; retained in schools as servant, 1; not known, 3'. (*Southern Star*, 9 November 1895)

Lawrence Collection

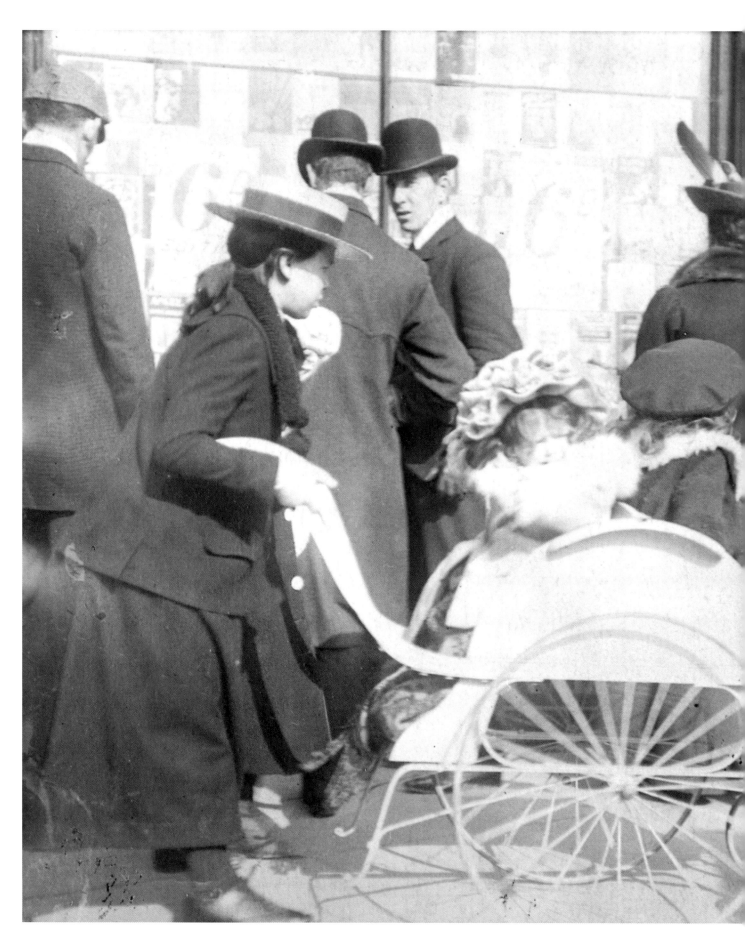

c. 1897

Grafton Street, Dublin

Perambulator for Two. Out and about on Grafton Street, this unusual back-to-back perambulator for two has caught the photographer's eye. This style of pram, called a mail-cart, was based on hand-carts used by the postal service.

Clarke Collection

1897 | Waterford

Photographer's Children. Violet Poole and her brother are helping their father with some experimental photography. As a photographer's children they were probably well used to posing and had mastered the art of staying still, yet looking relaxed and natural. It also must have been quite fun to pour water on the studio floor! The family is easily located in both the 1901 and 1911 census. Violet Beatrice was 13 in 1901. She is listed in the 1911 census, at the age of 23, as a photographer's assistant. The boy in the photograph is probably her younger brother, Vyvyan. Their father was Church of Ireland but the children were raised Catholic after their mother, as was common in mixed-denomination marriages.

A.H. Poole Collection

c. 1899 | Tramore, Co. Waterford

Dress-up. The baby and dog look equally muffled and ill at ease in their fancy outfits. Costumes for dogs were popular in the late nineteenth century although they usually took the form of human clothing rather than other animals. This appears to be a rabbit costume. Between the dog and baby, what looks like another animal is a lady's fur hand-muff.

A.H. Poole Collection

c. 1899

Galway

Real Irish Life. A romantic view of rural Ireland, invariably including donkeys, has long appealed to the tourist industry. This image, intended for the postcard trade, declares these two children with their donkey to be 'Real Irish' life.

Lawrence Collection

REAL IRISH. 5715. W. L.

47

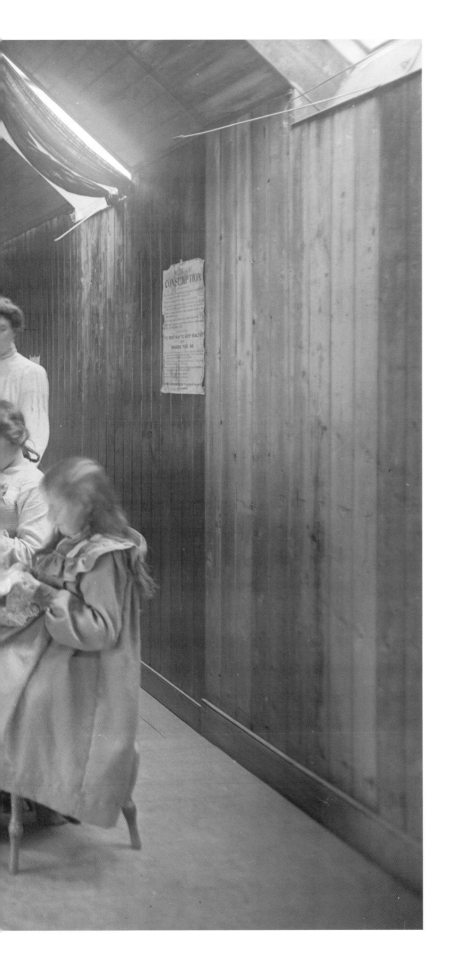

Donegal

Lace Making, Donegal. These girls are being taught to make crochet lace. Cottage industries, supported by the Congested Districts Board, helped families make extra money. The girls were paid a small weekly wage while learning their craft, and the items they made were sold in Dublin shops. Their labour made a small but significant contribution to their household incomes. A poster on the wall gives instructions 'To Prevent Consumption' (or tuberculosis as it is now better known).

Lawrence Collection

1899

Dunmore East, Co. Waterford

Ready to Play. Other photographs from the NLI's collection suggest that this is the Chapman family from Tramore, photographed here at what appears to be a holiday cottage in Dunmore East. The children have brought their fishing nets, toys and dog out onto the grass. Smocks, which had long been associated with shepherds, were introduced in the 1890s as less restrictive costume for children. Only the doll retains a more formal mode of dress. Dunmore East, where the photograph was taken, is still a popular holiday spot.

A.H. Poole Collection

c. 1900

Tramore,
Co. Waterford

Metal Man. One of three pillars built in 1823 to help prevent shipwrecks at Tramore, the Metal Man has made his way into local folklore. These girls are perhaps a bit young to be testing the belief that if you hopped barefoot around the Metal Man three times you would marry within the year.

Lawrence Collection

METAL MAN.TRAMORE.Co.WATERFORD.9054.W.L.

Enniscorthy, Co. Wexford

Mrs Davis as a Little Girl. Wearing a velvet coat and an elaborate winter bonnet, this little girl looks as though she should be on the front of a Christmas card. Labelled *Mrs Davis as a Little Girl*, it is likely that in the 1940s Mrs Davis had this photograph of herself as a young girl in the early 1900s re-photographed by the Poole Studio to preserve this endearing image. There is evidence of retouching along the top of her forehead where the photographer has filled in some hair.

A.H. Poole Collection

53

20 October 1900 | Ballinakill, Co. Laois

Hold Still! Baby Dobbyn looks a little apprehensive about having her photograph taken. Getting young children to stay still yet look relaxed would have been a challenge for the photographer. The length of exposures could be up to three seconds, an impossibly long time for a toddler. Modern cameras routinely take three frames per second, freezing time.

A.H. Poole Collection

c. 1903 | Waterford

'and smile ...' Baby Graves is a little more at ease with the camera and manages a smile. Smiling became possible (owing to reduced exposure times) and acceptable in photography in the early part of the twentieth century.

A.H. Poole Collection

c. 1900

York Street, Castleblayney, Co. Monaghan

Walking Home. This group of children have not noticed the photographer taking their picture as they walk home, sharing some food. From the expressions on their faces it looks like it might be toffee. It is likely the camera was held at waist level to avoid detection. The early 1900s saw the introduction of cheaper, portable cameras suitable for amateur enthusiasts. These cameras allowed for greater spontaneity and opportunism in capturing candid images.

Clarke Collection

c. 1900

Killarney, Co. Kerry

Cooperage. A family-run cooperage was in operation on Old Market Road in Killarney into the early 1900s. Before the widespread use of plastic containers, wooden barrels and containers were used for storing goods and to carry out a range of household activities such as laundry. Some of the barrels are held together with hazel withies rather than metal bands. A sack worn as a cape was good protection against the elements.

Lawrence Collection

c. 1901

Unknown

Baby's First Pony. Sitting on his pony, strapped into a basket saddle and holding a bouquet of flowers, this baby looks rather puzzled. His parents are obviously very proud of their first son. Basket saddles, which are still manufactured today, allow very young children to sit on a horse unaided.

A.H. Poole Collection

Unknown

Seesaw. An improvised seesaw, made from a log and a plank of wood, is put to more exciting use by the young boy on the left who has decided to walk along its length, thrilling and frightening himself in equal parts. It is imperative his big brother stays where he is for his mission to be a success!

Dixon Album

c. 1902 | Unknown

Farm Yard. This bucolic scene of children perched on top of an overloaded hay wagon would perhaps cause consternation today. In the background, clothes are draped over the lime-washed dry-stone wall and in the shadow of the hay the outline of a hen can be seen. In the early 1900s farming was still dependent on the horse for transport and ploughing. Horses continued to be used by many for decades to come, but by the 1940s their numbers were on the decrease as tractors became more prevalent.

Dixon Album

10 October 1902

De La Salle, Park Road, Waterford

The Ideal Classroom. This large classroom of forty-four boys is hard at work. Classroom sizes were often this large, although it is possible they were all put together for the photograph. The classroom has every conceivable learning aid. The walls are covered in maps, science diagrams and other educational aids. The classroom also boasts a typewriter, piano and fiddle. The text on the blackboard reveals that they were being taught Irish, a subject only approved for the curriculum in 1900.

A.H. Poole Collection

c. 1903 | Unknown

Don't know where to look! These young boys don't seem to know quite where to look when called upon to pose. The stick lying across the traditional basket (creel) was probably used to chivvy the donkey along, although he must have been reasonably obedient and used to his work as there is no halter or rope to be seen.

Dixon Album

c. 1903

Horse-drawn baby-carriage. Novelty perambulators based on horse-drawn carriages were popular in the late nineteenth century. In addition to full-sized models, fully working versions were made as toys. They can also be seen as props in studio photographs.

Clarke Collection

c. 1903 | Dugort, Achill, Co. Mayo

Cottage Industry. This young girl has brought her spinning wheel outdoors to take advantage of the natural light. Leaning up against the cottage wall is a quern stone, used to grind grain to make flour for bread. Rocks hold down the thatch, helping it resist the buffeting Atlantic winds.

Valentine Collection

c. 1903 | Galway

The Gardener's Girls. Photographed with their Jack Russell dog, these two little girls are identified as the Quinn children in the Clonbrock Album. The estate's gardener was named Quinn and had five daughters and two sons. It is likely that the little girls, as well as acting as photographic models, attended a school set up by the Dillon family.

Clonbrock Collection

c. 1902

Galway

Estate School. Mr James Gildea and Miss Annie Crowe with their classes at the school set up by Lord Clonbrock. Education, although compulsory, was not always well attended and may have proved too costly for some families. Charitable schools such as that supported by the Dillons provided education for those who otherwise could not afford it.

Clonbrock Collection

5 September 1906

John's Hill, Waterford

Sisters? Deciding if a child is a boy or a girl in a photograph dating from before the 1920s can be difficult. This brother and sister from Waterford are shown in typical clothing for children in the early twentieth century. Props and poses were used to differentiate between the genders in art and photographs. Boys were shown in active poses and with appropriate toys. This boy is standing and has been given a toy animal, while his sister is seated and holds a doll.

A.H. Poole Collection

6 October 1904 | Ferrybank, Wexford

Studio Toys. It must have been quite a wrench for some children to leave behind the delightful accessories of the photographer's studio. Dolls, stuffed animals, swings and novelty perambulators were all used to distract, entertain and placate young sitters.

A.H. Poole Collection

c. 1907 | Tramore, Co. Waterford

Tramore Beach. Everyone else seems to have abandoned the beach and left these children to their digging. In the background can be seen the bathing machines, lined up as though stored for winter.

A.H. Poole Collection

c. 1907

Newgrange, Co. Meath

Newgrange. Newgrange passage tomb is one of Ireland's most important and oldest archaeological sites. This photograph was taken some sixty years before the excavation that uncovered the roof box, through which the winter solstice sun lights up the ancient tomb.

Tempest Collection

3 April 1908

Ursuline Convent, Waterford

Easy and Graceful. Exercise formed an important part of the school day in the early 1900s. Movements were often set to music and were not overly exerting; some were designed to be done while sitting at a desk.

A.H. Poole Collection

79

16 June 1910

Waterpark College,
Park Road, Waterford

Cyclists. These Waterpark boys are dressed (undressed?) for exercise in their vests and underpants.

A.H. Poole Collection

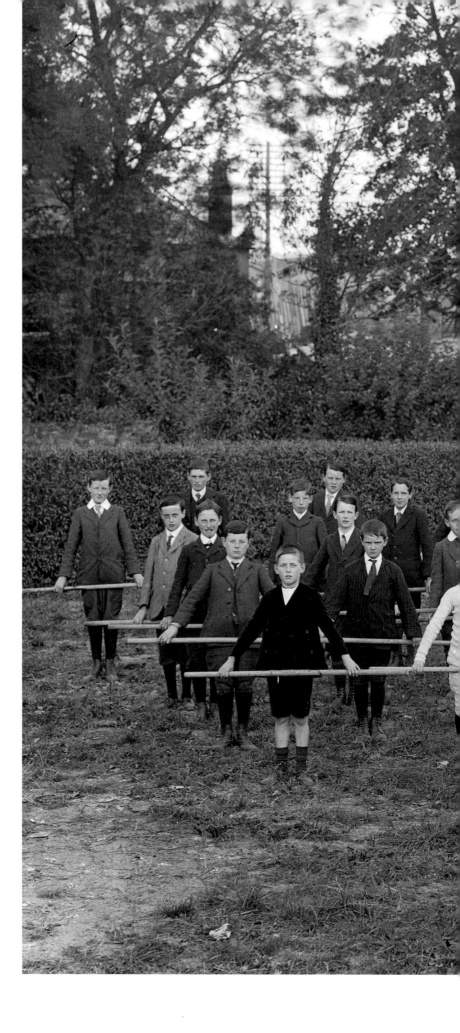

c. 1910

Waterpark College, Park Road, Waterford

Dress as Loosely as Possible. This teacher from Waterpark College has neglected to read *Simple Lessons in Physical Drill*, published for the use of national schools in 1909. The book advises that during exercise, 'the unfastening of a button on the coat or waistcoat or at the neck may often be desirable'.

A.H. Poole Collection

c. 1908

Waterford

Fortune Teller. Fancy dress, or perhaps amateur theatricals, take on a new twist with the addition of roller-skates. Roller-skating gained popularity in the late nineteenth century with the invention of the four-wheeled skate. Around the country, ballrooms saw new use as roller-skating rinks.

A.H. Poole Collection

c. 1908 | Louth

Sandbag. Dressed in a fashionable sailor suit, Trevor helps his mother fill a sack with sand from the beach, a practice that has been illegal since the 1930s. Hopefully the sand was not intended for use in a garden, as the salt content of the sea-sand would not have been good for the plants.

Tempest Collection

c. 1910

Connemara, Galway

Congested Districts. In equal parts intrigued by and uninterested in the man behind the camera, it is possible that these children don't even realise they are having their photograph taken. Images such as this one could be used by the Congested Districts Board in slideshows to highlight the poverty of western Ireland to concerned philanthropists in Dublin and beyond.

Congested Districts Board Collection

c. 1910

Connemara, Galway

Big Sister. Carrying her younger sibling on her back while she strides along barefoot, this girl is seemingly oblivious to the uneven, rocky ground underfoot.

Congested Districts Board Collection

Unknown

Mission Stall. A young girl sets up a mission
stall selling rosary beads and religious statues,
while her young friends help.

Eason Collection

c. 1912

Unknown

Turf Carrier. This boy is carefully dressed in a shirt, waistcoat and jacket. Closer examination reveals his clothing to be a patchwork of repairs. Before the mass production of synthetic fabrics, clothing was expensive and not easily or wantonly replaced.

Eason Collection

c. 1913

Waterford

School Photo. Dressed in their best for their school photo, these young boys are wearing a mix of the ever-popular sailor suit and more contemporary high-necked jumpers. The shoes are also a mix of traditional and new. Some of the boys are wearing side-buttoned boots, which were more common between 1880 and 1900, while others wear laced boots; just one boy that we can see wears white socks and fashionable strap shoes. Scuffed knees and holes in socks add character to an otherwise very posed studio shot.

A.H. Poole Collection

21 February 1917

Unknown

Irish Guards. The Irish Guards have had an Irish Wolfhound as a mascot since 1902. In 1917 *Leitrim Boy* retired and *Doran* took over duties. The mascot was cared for by a drummer boy, seen here dressed in service dress. He wears ankle boots and puttees. Puttees are long lengths of wool cloth wound around the calf to protect the lower leg.

A.H. Poole Collection

c. 1917

Unknown

Na Fianna Éireann. Military-style youth organisations for boys were popular throughout Europe in the early 1900s. They emphasised discipline, health and pride in their nation's history. Na Fianna Éireann, otherwise known as the Irish National Boy Scouts, was established in 1909 by Countess Markievicz. The 1917 handbook, with contributions by Sir Roger Casement on 'Chivalry' and Pádraig Pearse on the history of the 'Fianna of the Fionn', outlines the main activities of the organisation, including drill, signalling, camp life, swimming, rifle exercises and — as seen in the photograph — first aid.

Keogh Collection

22 August 1920

Templemore, Co. Tipperary

Bleeding Statues. During the War of Independence, local people believed that a miracle had stopped Templemore from being completely destroyed during a reprisal attack by the Black and Tans. Statues of the Virgin Mary were said to have begun bleeding while the town was being attacked, and over the coming days miracle cures were reported. The statues were brought to Dwan's shop, where a makeshift altar was erected. A reported 15,000 people a day came to pray at the statues.

W.D. Hogan Collection

22 August 1920

Templemore, Co. Tipperary

Repairs. A house in Templemore requires boarding up in the aftermath of the reprisal raid by the Northamptonshire Regiment and Black and Tans. With its broken window, this house has escaped the worst of the damage visited on the town during the night of 16 August, which saw looting, gunfire and parts of the town burned, destroying homes and businesses.

Hogan-Wilson Collection

1922

Four Courts, Dublin

Playing at Rebels. Two boys walk past the sandbagged gates of the Four Courts during its occupation by anti-Treaty forces. One boy holds a toy gun, the other a hurley, as a makeshift rifle. A British Pathé newsreel described the scene: '[E]ven miniature soldiers "play rebels" in front of the sandbag fortifications at Four Courts.'

Fitzelle Album

June 1922

Lower Baggot Street, Dublin

The arrival of the Free State forces has drawn a crowd to Ferguson's garage. The garage was raided by anti-Treaty forces in an attempt to commandeer cars which had been illegally purchased in Belfast, in defiance of the Belfast Boycott. The children, caught up in the general excitement of events, have turned their attention from the armoured car to the photographer.

Fitzelle Album

c. 1922

Cork

Barricades. The immersion of young people in the events they are surrounded by is forcibly illustrated by this image of a pair of young teenagers, one armed with a .303 Lee Enfield rifle. They appear to be searching the horse-drawn bread van. Although it is likely that this photograph was staged for the benefit of the photographer, the barricades across the street, visible in the background, attest to the tense situation in the city during the Civil War.

W.D. Hogan Collection

1922

Dublin

Children Play Red Cross. Children's games often reflect what they see around them. Here the children are acting out what must have been a familiar scene in Dublin during the Civil War.

Independent Newspapers (Ireland) Limited

111

August 1922

Cork

Salvage. A barefoot boy holds a sword salvaged from Victoria Barracks (now Collins Barracks) after its evacuation and burning by Republicans. Burning rendered the barracks useless to the advancing Free State troops and provided opportunity for looting for local people.

Hogan-Wilson Collection

March 1922

Cork

Bouquet. Children are often called upon to meet with famous people. Here a young boy offers a bouquet — almost as large as himself — to Michael Collins.

Hogan-Wilson Collection

28 August 1922

Dublin

Michael Collins's Funeral. Na Fianna Éireann carry wreaths as part of the funeral procession of Michael Collins. Hundreds of thousands lined the route of the procession. The boys' uniform comprised kilts and Tara brooches. The kilt, although not a true national costume, was adopted by cultural revivalists as a symbol of Ireland's 'Celtic' heritage.

Independent Newspapers (Ireland) Limited

15 May 1924

Ursuline Convent, Waterford

The Dolls' Hospital. The pupils of the Ursuline Convent are dressed as babies, soldiers, Japanese dolls; others are dressed as nurses to care for them.

A.H. Poole Collection

c. 1924

Dublin

Children's Party. The note on the back of this photograph says, 'Party given by gentlemen to children, Dublin'. Among the very enthusiastic children can be seen a gentlemen dressed, pantomime fashion, as a dame.

W.D. Hogan Collection

2 February 1924

Alexander Street, Waterford

Lean-to Home. Eviction was not confined to a rural context in Ireland. By the 1920s, unemployment and failure to pay rent saw many families without a home. This photograph was taken at the behest of a Mrs E. White who campaigned for better measures of relief for the unemployed.

A.H. Poole Collection

c. 1924

Arran Street, Dublin

St Patrick's Day. A group of dancers, taught by a Miss Forde, prepare for St Patrick's Day festivities in Dublin. The business name on the wall plaque suggests that they are in the Smithfield area of the city. Stuck into the garlanded fence is a small flag featuring a harp.

W.D. Hogan Collection

30 May 1928

Waterford

Kindergarten Class. The Kindergarten approach to education was advocated from the early 1900s. This approach emphasised the importance of learning through play, art and other interactive activities, rather than simply learning by rote.

A.H. Poole Collection

8 July 1929

Cork

Distracted. A young girl finds it difficult to keep her eyes on the Blessed Sacrament as it passes along a street in Cork. The procession is part of centenary celebrations of Catholic Emancipation in 1829. Emancipation repealed the last of the penal laws which had been in place since the seventeenth century. Those laws had greatly circumscribed the ability of Catholics to participate in business and public life.

Independent Newspapers (Ireland) Limited

2 September 1930

Mount Congreve, Kilmeadan, Co. Waterford

Charity Play. These boys are taking part in a play to raise money for local charities, organised by Lady Irene Graham of Mount Congreve. The rehearsals were reported in the local press, which names two of the boys: 'Master Patrick Baring is seated on the wheelbarrow, and next to him is Master Charles Blacque, son of General and the Hon Mrs Blacque …' (*Irish Independent*, 30 September 1930).

A.H. Poole Collection

2 September 1930

Mount Congreve, Kilmeadan, Co. Waterford

Cooks. This is the same group of boys as in the Charity Play. Unfortunately no script has survived which might explain their being dressed as gardeners and cooks.

A.H. Poole Collection

c. 1930 | Waterford

Fancy Dress. Harking back to an earlier time, this young boy is dressed in a costume inspired by eighteenth-century fashions. The most likely explanation for his costume is that he is participating in amateur theatricals.

A.H. Poole Collection

1 June 1932 | Passage Road, Waterford

Theatrical Group. Students from St John of God Convent School in Waterford portray St Patrick surrounded by angels, monks and characters from Irish folklore.

A.H. Poole Collection

1932

Dublin

The Walls of Limerick. Here we see the good-
natured chaos of a large group of children
rehearsing their dancing, in this case for the
Eucharistic Congress celebrations. They
appear to be dancing 'The Walls of Limerick',
a dance for sets of two couples. After
advancing and retiring, the couples swap
sides by exchanging diagonally with their
counterparts. Then they spin — officially for
one turn so as to face a new couple, but often
energy and enthusiasm overwhelm
technique.

Independent Newspapers (Ireland) Limited

26 June 1932

Phoenix Park, Dublin

A Welcome Drink. One hundred thousand people attended an open-air Mass in the Phoenix Park, Dublin, during the 31st Eucharistic Congress in June 1932. A Boy Scout gives a young girl, wearing her First Holy Communion dress, a drink of water. Hundreds of Boy Scouts assisted at the event, directing the crowds and administering first aid.

Independent Newspapers (Ireland) Limited

21 September 1933 | Leperstown, Waterford

Mrs Flynn, Leperstown. In September 1933 nine Waterford farmers were arrested for failure to pay rates. Their arrest and incarceration became national news and the farmers were eventually released. In this sequence of four images the photographer emphasises the plight of a family left without a father.

A.H. Poole Collection

21 September 1933 | Kilmacleague, Co. Waterford

Mrs Cullinane, Kilmacleague.

A.H. Poole Collection

21 September 1933 | Rathmoylan, Co. Waterford

Mrs William O'Brien, Rathmoylan.

A.H. Poole Collection

21 September 1933

Brownstown, Co. Waterford

Mrs Hally, Brownstown. A newspaper report notes that Mr Hally was 'temporarily released for domestic reasons' (*Irish Press*, 9 September 1933).

A.H. Poole Collection

15 August 1935

Mount Loftus, Powerstown, Co. Kilkenny

Wedding Party. The *Irish Press* reported on Miss P. Loftus's wedding to Commander Bayliss, describing the children's outfits: 'pages Master D. and L. O'Brien dressed as huntsmen, Misses S. Dobbs and E. Fowler, as bridesmaids, in early French hunting costumes' (*Irish Press*, 16 August 1935).

A.H. Poole Collection

14 November 1935

Arranmore, Co. Donegal

Arranmore Disaster. Nineteen people (including seven members of one family) from Arranmore Island, off the coast of Donegal, lost their lives in a boating accident on 9 November 1935. They were travelling home to their small island community from Scotland, where they had worked the potato harvest. Their open sailing boat (yawl) capsized after hitting a submerged rock just a few hundred metres from shore. There was only one survivor. The ruined buildings in the background add to the sense of loss visible in the boys' faces as they trudge up the slope towards the photographer.

Independent Newspapers (Ireland) Limited

31 May 1936

Kerry

Irish Dancers. Varying degrees of apprehension, seriousness and enthusiasm are visible in the faces of these children, asked to perform at the opening of the Fitzgerald Memorial Park in Kerry, which was named for Dick Fitzgerald, a renowned Kerry footballer. The official opening was attended by 40,000 visitors. One girl is out of time with her companions, while another directs her attention to the photographer. Their dancing costumes are simple compared with today's heavily embroidered dresses, although the beginnings can be seen in the Tara brooches and capes. Soft shoes, which were introduced in 1924, are worn by all but one of the dancers.

Independent Newspapers (Ireland) Limited

c. 1937 | Unknown

Doll's House. What young girl wouldn't be proud of a doll's house that is almost bigger than herself? Built in mock-Tudor style, this is a thoroughly modern house, complete with garage, although one of the doors has gone missing. The front walls of the house are painted with climbing plants.

O'Dea Album

c. 1937 | Unknown

Kitten. A young girl takes her nursing duties very seriously when charged with the care of a motherless kitten. Thankfully, the understandably curious dog is safely contained behind the gate.

O'Dea Album

1937

Dublin Zoo

Saying Hello. This little girl is being introduced to a donkey at Dublin Zoo in the Phoenix Park. At first glance she looks as though she might be afraid of the donkey. But it turns out her mother has given her some bread for the donkey and she has decided to eat it herself! According to the *Irish Independent,* 20 January 1937, which featured this photograph, 'This is the only pet donkey ever secured by a zoo from a Gipsy troop. It is a great favourite with the children …' It is unlikely the children knew that, just a few years before, the same newspaper reported that during a typical year '31 donkeys' formed part of the 'varied dishes' offered to the animals.

Independent Newspapers (Ireland) Limited

1937 | Broadstone, Dublin

Picnic. Protected by picnic blankets, the toddlers take a reluctant nap. Their father, a railway enthusiast, travelled the length and breadth of Ireland taking pictures of trains and railways.

O'Dea Album

1938 | Derryaroge, Co. Kildare

Look This Way. A guiding pair of hands either side of a head, and a strategically restraining hand to the shoulder, ensure that all of the children face the right way to have their picture taken!

O'Dea Album

31 May 1939

Aran Islands, Co. Galway

Aran Island Girls. These girls are wearing a variety of traditional Aran clothing which would not have been out of place half a century before: pampooties, crios belts and cross-over shawls. Pampooties are simple shoes made from a single piece of cow-hide, punched with holes around the upper edge and laced over the foot with leather thonging. A crios is a wide hand-woven belt. To make a belt, the weaver attaches threads to their foot/shoe and finger-weaves the multi-coloured wool threads, creating a regular pattern, usually edged with white.

Independent Newspapers (Ireland) Limited

c. 1940 | Kerry

Summer Dress. Wearing what appear to be home-made summer dresses, these two young girls seem in equal parts delighted and nervous about having their photograph taken.

Album 396

1940 | Clondalkin, Dublin

Railway Children. A hundred years after the boom in railway building, rail travel still formed an important part of the transport network in Ireland into the late 1940s. Towards the end of the decade, diesel began to replace steam. Increased use of road motor-vehicles saw the decline of railways and the closure of many railway stations, as passengers gave way to freight and there was no need to call at every station.

O'Dea Album

GENTOURS BOYS CAMP, SKERRIES.

VR.2900.

c. 1940

Skerries, Co. Dublin

Holiday Camp. Gentours Boys' Camp in Skerries was run by the Dowling family. Chalets eventually replaced the tents.

Valentine Collection

May 1941

Dublin

The Emergency. The accidental bombing of the North Strand by the Luftwaffe in May 1941 resulted in considerable damage and the loss of many lives, including seven children aged between three months and seven years. The full death toll remains unknown, with estimates ranging from twenty-eight to thirty-four people killed or dying from injuries sustained during the bombing.

Independent Newspapers (Ireland) Limited

31 October 1942 | Carrick-on-Suir, Co. Tipperary

Hollywood. There is something of the Hollywood starlet in the style of the young girl on the right.

A.H. Poole Collection

February 1943 | Dublin

Johnny Forty Coats. A young boy chats with Johnny Forty Coats. One of Dublin's street characters, P.J. Marlow gained the name 'Forty Coats' owing to his habit of wearing several coats at once, regardless of the season.

Independent Newspapers (Ireland) Limited

c. 1947

Unknown

The Other Side. Photographers are not often seen on the other side of the camera. Here W.D. Hogan, who was responsible for the striking images from the Civil War period, poses with a friend's family in 1947.

W.D. Hogan

23 November 1949

Waterford

Lámha Suas. Christmas has come early to this classroom of girls in Waterford. In the background, a cheery cardboard cut-out Santa Claus is decorated with balloons.

A.H. Poole Collection

c. 1950

Unknown

School Yard. Lunch time in the school yard, the realm of hide-and-go-seek, kiss chasing, Red Rover, skipping, chasing, and best friends whispering in corners.

Cardall Collection

1950

Cappagh, Co. Waterford

The Cashman Family. Professional portraiture continued to be popular even with the availability of cheap, easy-to-use cameras. In the hundred years since the advent of studio photographic portraiture, the enthusiasm of young subjects may have been unchanged, but their clothing, and the nature of photography, had changed utterly. No longer is it a guessing game to figure out who is a boy or a girl. Their clothing, although distinctly gendered, is simple and less restrictive than that of their forebears; they even wear shoes without socks.

A.H. Poole Collection

24 August 1953

Bosheen, New Ross, Co. Wexford

Travelling Studio. The scuffed surface of the studio floor may indicate that this is a portable studio set up at a country fair or similar. The children all appear to be holding their own toys, rather than ones provided by the studio.

A.H. Poole Collection

c. 1953

Derry

Springtown Camp. One of the 'tin-towns' that were occupied by squatters after WWII. Tin-towns were abandoned army and naval bases comprising wooden and metal huts (Nissen huts). Vacated by American soldiers, they were quickly occupied by young couples attempting to start new lives in homes of their own after the war. Conditions quickly deteriorated, as temporary accommodation became permanent homes for hundreds of families.

Colman Doyle

1953 | Essex Street, Dublin

Cowboy. A young boy chalks a cowboy onto a
wall on Essex Street. American cowboy films were
extremely popular throughout the 1940s and
1950s. Going to the 'pictures' could take up a
whole afternoon as many local cinemas offered
double-bills — targeted at children — with a
specially priced ticket. Serialisations that ended on
a cliffhanger ensured the children returned week
after week to discover the fate of their heroes.

Wiltshire Collection

1954 | Dublin

Who's She? Two little boys give model Linda O'Reilly an appraising look as she is photographed on a Dublin street.

Colman Doyle

1954 | Loughrea, Co. Galway

Sheridan/O'Brien Camp. Pictured at the family
site in Galway in front of a traditional caravan,
these two boys from the Travelling Community
happily pose for the camera. Despite their worn
clothes they are both wearing ties. Braces help to
keep up their hand-me-down trousers.

Wiltshire Collection

13 June 1954 | Ballycullen, Rathfarnham, Dublin

Interrupted at Prayer. The piercing stare of this young girl makes the photographer's intrusion on a private moment of contemplation all the more obvious. The group is praying at St Columcille's Well in Dublin. Holy wells have been part of Irish worship since pre-Christian times.

Wiltshire Collection

1954

York Street, Dublin

Their Whole World. During summer months the cramped conditions of the Dublin city tenements could be alleviated somewhat by sending the children outdoors to play for the day. The paths in front of the houses were as much a part of their homes as the one or two rooms they inhabited.

Wiltshire Collection

1963 | Dunganstown, Co. Wexford

Meeting JFK. President John F. Kennedy gives his full attention to a young girl during a visit to his family's ancestral home in Dunganstown in June 1963. While one girl has her hands casually stuffed into her pockets, another, perhaps a little overwhelmed by the occasion and meeting such an illustrious person, has her hands clasped as though in prayer.

Colman Doyle

1964 | Quays, Dublin

Don't Fall. Something has intrigued the children enough for them to lean precariously over the wall of the River Liffey. The swans have also been disturbed and paddle to the centre of the river.

Wiltshire Collection

1964 | Dublin

Grand Canal. From the eighteenth century, and before the advent of rail travel, networks of canals were the main transport arteries for freight in Ireland. They continued in this capacity until the 1960s, when they fell into disuse. A long period of neglect has ended with a welcome regeneration for some canals. Tow paths are now used as cycle and walking routes. Working boats have been transformed into floating holiday homes.

Wiltshire Collection

1964 | Seapoint, Dublin

Martello Tower. This seaside scene is a marked contrast to earlier photographs of children enjoying a day at the beach. Their casual clothes, or lack of them, and their unsupervised play show a freedom unimaginable sixty years before.

Wiltshire Collection

1964 | York Street, Dublin

Tenement Evictions. Families protest against their
eviction from the York Street tenements. A
cardboard sign on the railings reads 'God Bless
the Corporation', another reads 'Children
Homeless'. Although tenement life was cramped
and many of the buildings were in such disrepair
that some had collapsed, families still considered
them home, and were reluctant to leave.

Wiltshire Collection

1964 | Ballsbridge, Dublin

Wandering Goat. An unlikely visitor to urban
Dublin intrigues two young girls. The iconic item of
clothing of the 1960s may have been the mini-skirt,
but the decade also saw acceptance of trousers as
suitable clothing for girls. Notwithstanding attempts
to make women's trousers fashionable in previous
decades, they were generally only thought
acceptable as sportswear or workwear.

Wiltshire Collection

1964 | St Stephen's Green, Dublin

Summer Sun. Soaking up the summer sun in St Stephen's Green. Until the late 1870s St Stephen's Green, in common with other city parks, was only for the use of wealthy residents. The move towards public parks began in the nineteenth century. At a time when much of the population still lived in city centres, rather than in outer suburbs, public parks were an attempt by local authorities to improve the health of the populace, giving them respite from the dirt and bustle of the cities.

Wiltshire Collection

1966 | Arbour Hill, Dublin

Memorial. Photographed in front of the memorial of the 1916 Easter Rising, the little girls look as though they might be reading the engraved text of the Proclamation of the Republic, 'cherishing all the children of the nation equally'.

Wiltshire Collection

1969 | Sandymount, Dublin

Balancing Act. A poised young girl removes herself from the crowded beach.

Wiltshire Collection

1969 | Sandymount, Dublin

Sea-creatures. Almost a century after Clarke took his image of two fully-clad girls tentatively paddling in the sea (on pages 34–5), Elinor Wiltshire captured this image of two young girls intently hunting for sea-creatures in a shallow pool at low tide. Trousers, jumpers and short cotton skirts have taken the place of the hats and bloomers of the early twentieth century.

Wiltshire Collection

June 1969

Manor Street, Dublin

Communion Girls. A group of girls wearing their communion dresses form part of a Corpus Christi procession in Dublin. The young nun and her charges participating in this traditional religious practice are contrasted with the fashionable teenagers, leaning against the wall. Youth culture had permeated Ireland in the 1960s although tradition still held sway over much of daily life.

Wiltshire Collection

1969 | Coleraine Street, Dublin

Eager Models. Squashing up against the railings in their eagerness to have their photograph taken, these young children are pictured outside the Coleraine Street flats in Dublin which have been decorated with bunting for Corpus Christi celebrations.

Wiltshire Collection

1969 | Moore Street, Dublin

Donation. There is a grown-up feeling about putting money into the plate at Mass, or into a charity box.

Wiltshire Collection

1969 | Cumberland Street, Dublin

A Place to Read. Sitting in a tea chest is one way to get away from a busy marketplace and enjoy a book. Cumberland Street market is still held every Saturday.

Wiltshire Collection

Wiltshire Collection

1969 | Cumberland Street, Dublin

Comics. At time when many homes had black and white televisions — if they had one at all — a colourful world of escape was offered by comics. They could be bought for a few pence out of pocket money, and shared and swapped with friends.

September 1969 | Belfast

Peace Line. A little girl, whose entire focus is on having her photograph taken, is starkly juxtaposed with the removal of a barricade constructed in the aftermath of intensive rioting in Belfast. Some of the barricades were to remain and become the foundations for 'peace lines'.

Independent Newspapers (Ireland) Limited

June 1969 | Henrietta Street, Dublin

Posing for the Camera. A young girl enjoys the sunshine during the Corpus Christi festival. Henrietta Street is one of Dublin's oldest Georgian streets. At the time they were built, in the early eighteenth century, the large houses were home to the wealthy and fashionable. In the late nineteenth century these once desirable properties became tenements for the working classes. Where one family had lived in luxury, now dozens of families lived in crowded and deteriorating conditions. Henrietta Street remained as tenements until the 1970s.

Wiltshire Collection

1969

Ballymun, Dublin

Skipping. The Ballymun flats in north County Dublin were built in 1966 as part of a plan to move families out of the crowded city centre and the seriously dilapidated tenement buildings. The modern buildings with their relatively spacious apartments fitted with modern plumbing, central heating and electricity, combined with space for children to play, were, at the time, a relief from tenement life for many. The move, however, was not without difficulty: close-knit city-centre communities were broken up in the dispersal to the suburbs. Long-term problems arose from the inadequate provision of amenities for the dramatically increased population. The area has undergone a further regeneration and only one of the original seven iconic tower blocks remains standing.

Wiltshire Collection

1970

Unknown

Public House. Red lemonade and a packet of crisps would have been the usual fare of children brought to an Irish pub in the 1970s.

Galbraith Collection

1970

Limerick

Battleground. The adults are giving a wide berth to these boys playing in an alleyway with water pistols.

Galbraith Collection

1970

Unknown

Home in Time for Dinner. We can imagine that
these two young boys, casting long shadows as
they cycle along the footpath accompanied by
their faithful hound, are heading home after a
busy day of play.

Galbraith Collection

THE COLLECTIONS

The photographs in *Small Lives* are drawn from the following collections at the National Library of Ireland. The NLI houses about 4.5 million photographs covering all aspects of Irish life, from the beginnings of photography in Ireland in the 1840s to the present day. The collection comprises the largest single body of photographs of Irish interest in the world, and is an invaluable visual record. To date, approximately 40,000 photos from the collections can be viewed on the NLI catalogue, *www.nli.ie*.

A.H. Poole

The A.H. Poole Photographic Collection consists of photos taken by the family firm of A.H. Poole in Waterford during the period 1884–1954. This collection consists of 65,000 glass negatives. The majority of the collection consists of portraits of Waterford people. This would include studio portraits of local individuals, group portraits of business firms, school classes, clubs and societies. Other subjects include images of Waterford life and development: turkeys being brought to market, The Quay; Reginald's Tower and the Quay; Granville Hotel, Meagher's Quay; fife and drum band; torpedo boats at the Quay; coal at docks, Mr Murphy's, Ferrybank; motor cars in Manor Street; Tramore Strand, and many more. In addition to Waterford city and county, other areas covered include Wexford, Kilkenny and Cork. The collection also includes some postcard views such as individualised postcards for local firms and other institutions.

Album 200

A *carte de visite* album belonging to the Edgeworth family depicting family members; not all sitters are identified. Includes family members wearing traditional Chinese clothing. With some religious cards.

Album 396

Featuring photographs of West Kerry and the Blasket Islands, including views of the coastline and beaches, cottages, farms, harvesting crops with horse-drawn machinery, fishing, currach racing from Dunquin to the Blaskets, and a portrait of Peig Sayers seated by her fireplace. Also included are views of Dublin, notably the barges and sail boats on the River Liffey, the Custom House, Ha'penny Bridge, Nelson's Pillar and O'Connell Street and Henry Street, taken from the top of Nelson's Pillar. The photographer, Tomás O'Muircheartaigh, worked as a civil servant in the Department of Education. He was active in Conradh na Gaeilge, serving as its president 1955–9. His chief interest and spare-time occupation was photographing life in the west of Ireland: the people, customs and landscapes.

Album 426

The Domville family album. Studio portraits, mounted and with captions, of members of the Domville family, of Santry, Co. Dublin, and members of the Doyle family, the Domvilles' friends, and neighbours and employees. Also included are scrapbook items, including humorous and religious cards.

Album 97

Carte de visite portraits of members of the Fortescue family of Stephenstown House, Co. Louth, with many identified and dated on verso (includes Irish regiments). Includes some sitters in army uniform.

Album 98

Carte de visite portraits of members of the Fortescue family of Stephenstown House, Co. Louth, with many identified and dated on verso (includes Irish regiments). Includes some sitters in army uniform.

Cardall

Primarily a collection of 5,000 black and white photographic prints (postcards) of urban views in Ireland, dating from 1940 to 1960. The collection also includes a series of 150 unidentified film negatives which appear to be personal family photographs.

Clonbrock

The Clonbrock Collection contains 3,500 glass negatives, about 300 glass lantern slides, and one album of 71 photographic prints, spanning the years 1860–1930. The photographers were members of the Dillon family, Barons Clonbrock, of Ahascragh, Co. Galway, a family of enthusiastic amateur photographers. The images provide a substantial and varied pictorial record of life on a landed estate and of the family's travels to neighbouring estates and to London.

Colman Doyle

Colman Doyle is the award-winning photographer who worked with the *Irish Press* from 1950 to 2000. Comprising 28,000 prints covering politics, social history, portraits, sport and the Troubles in Northern Ireland, the collection represents almost sixty years of Doyle's career as a photographer with the *Irish Press* and *Paris Match*. Colman Doyle officially presented his entire photographic collection to the NLI in 2006.

Congested Districts Board

A collection of photographs dating from 1906 to 1914, comprising 120 photographic prints. Most of the photos were taken by the well-known Belfast photographer Robert J. Welch. The photographs document life in the congested districts along the western coast. The Congested Districts Board was established in 1891 and the work continued until 1923, when the Land Commission took over its functions.

Coolgreany

The Coolgreany Eviction Album documents the eviction of families on the Brooke estate at Coolgreany, near Gorey, Co. Wexford, in 1887.

Dixon

A family album depicting the children and friends of the Dixon family from 1900 to 1910.

Eason

This photographic collection consists of over 4,000 glass negatives created for the Irish views postcard trade by Eason & Son between 1900 and 1939.

Eblana

The Eblana Collection is a subset, comprising almost 3,000 glass negatives, of the Lawrence Collection and was probably purchased to augment the Lawrence postcard business. The eviction scenes are part of a larger collection of topographical views of various parts of Ireland between 1870 and 1890.

Fitzelle Album 135

The Fitzelle Album contains images taken during the Civil War of 1922, specifically Dublin and Limerick between May and July 1922. Most of the photographs were taken by W.D. Hogan, with official sanction. The majority depict Free State forces on active service.

Galbraith

James Galbraith began his career as a photographer for the US Air Force; later he worked for newspapers in Ann Arbor, Michigan as well as for other Michigan newspapers. In 2006, the National Photographic Archive (NPA) acquired a significant collection of 1,272 negatives and 131 prints taken by him during his visits to Ireland in 1970, 1978 and 1997. These images feature various aspects of Irish life that changed dramatically during a period spanning almost thirty years. In particular, the photographs provide insights into daily life in rural areas as well as in small towns and villages in Cork, Kerry and Clare.

Hogan-Wilson

The Hogan-Wilson Collection was acquired by the NLI in 2007 and comprises a set of photographs collected by the Rev. Denis Wilson, a chaplain to the national army, and mainly taken by W.D. Hogan, a commercial photographer based in Henry Street, Dublin between 1920 and 1935.

Independent Newspapers (Ireland) Limited

Comprising an estimated 4.3 million photographic negatives taken between 1905 and 2005 for the *Irish Independent* newspaper, the material in this collection is of immense historical value and provides an excellent record of almost every aspect of twentieth-century Irish life.

J.J. Clarke

Seventy-six images, showing Dubliners in the city between 1897 and 1904. The photographs were taken by medical student J.J. Clarke.

Keogh

The Keogh collection comprises 300 images, created by the Keogh Brothers of Dorset Street, Dublin. They provide excellent coverage of the political figures and events of 1915–23.

Lawrence

The Lawrence Collection consists of glass plate negatives covering the period 1870–1914. The images were produced commercially and capture scenes of that period throughout Ireland. The bulk of the outdoor images were taken by Robert French, the Lawrences' chief photographer.

O'Dea

The O'Dea Collection contains 5,350 photographs, covering all aspects of railway transport in Ireland between 1937 and 1966. The photographs were all taken by James P. O'Dea, a devoted railway enthusiast, and subjects include locomotives, railway stations and bridges, as well as railway staff and passengers.

Tempest

The Tempest family of Dundalk, Co. Louth operated a successful printing and stationery business in the town. The collection comprises images of the surrounding counties in the first decade of the twentieth century.

Tuke

This collection of photographs was taken by Major Rutledge Fair on behalf of philanthropist and social activist James Hack Tuke. Both men were deeply involved in trying to improve the lot of people living in the west of Ireland who were suffering from extreme poverty.

Valentine

Comprising images taken for the postcard trade, the Valentine Collection dates from 1929 to 1950.

W.D. Hogan

W.D. Hogan was a commercial and press photographer located in Henry Street, Dublin between 1920 and 1935. It is likely that Hogan took these 160 photographs under contract. The 5″ x 7″ black and white photographs show life in early June and July 1922 in Dublin during the early Civil War period, with armed and uniformed men on the streets.

Wiltshire Collection

The Wiltshire Collection (1951–71) consists of 322 photographic prints and 1,000 film negatives. The photographs were taken by Elinor O'Brien Wiltshire (1918–) and her husband Reginald Wiltshire (d.1968), owners of The Green Studios Ltd, Dublin (1958–68, St Stephen's Green; after 1968, Harcourt Street). Subjects include Travellers in Loughrea, Co. Galway and Buttevant, Co. Cork, 1954; Pattern Day in Rathfarnham, Co. Dublin, 1954; Moore Street market, 1964; demolitions at Charlotte Street, 1964 and Lower Fitzwilliam Street, 1965; Cumberland Street market, 1969; Corpus Christi parade, Halston Street, 1969; Sandymount Strand, 1969; and scenes along the banks of the Grand Canal. Events depicted include the demolition of Nelson's Pillar, 9 March 1966 and the York Street evictions, 1964. Also featured are many Dublin landmarks and street scenes such as the Five Lamps, Portland Row and O'Connell Street.

NLI Catalogue Reference Numbers

Page 1, *Album 97*; page 2, *Album 97*; page 3, *Album 426*; page 4, *Album 426*; page 5, *Lawrence Collection, L_CAB_01122*; page 6, *Clonbrock Collection, CLON176*; page 7, *Clonbrock Collection, CLON317*; page 8, *Album 200*; page 9, *Album 98*; pages 10–11, *Clonbrock Collection, CLON55*; page 12, *Clonbrock Collection, CLON66A*; page 13, *Album 200*; page 14, *Coolgreany Evictions Album, COOL886b*; page 15, *Eblana Collection, EB2659*; pages 16–17, *Lawrence Collection, L_CAB_04046*; page 18, *A.H. Poole Collection, POOLEIMP 144*; page 19, *Lawrence Collection, L_ROY_05092*; page 20, *A.H. Poole Collection, POOLEIMP 165*; page 21, *A.H. Poole Collection, POOLEIMP 236*; pages 22–3, *Lawrence Collection, L_CAB_08782*; pages 24–5, *Tuke Collection, TUKE35*; page 26, *Tuke Collection, TUKE38*; page 27, *Tuke Collection, TUKE37*; pages 28–9, *A.H. Poole Collection, POOLEIMP 414*; pages 30–31, *Irish Personalities List, BOX LXII, r_29987*; page 32, *A.H. Poole Collection, P_WP_1058*; page 33, *Lawrence Collection, L_ROY_02380*; pages 34–5, *Clarke Collection, CLAR39*; page 36, *Clarke Collection, CLAR29*; page 37, *Clarke Collection, CLAR41*; pages 38–9, *Clarke Collection, CLAR78*; page 40, *Lawrence Collection, L_ROY_02594*; page 41, *Lawrence Collection, L_CAB_05193*; pages 42–3, *Clarke Collection, CLAR15*; page 44, *A.H. Poole Collection, P_WP_0706*; page 45, *A.H. Poole Collection, P_WP_0789*; pages 46–7, *Lawrence Collection, L_CAB_05715*; pages 48–9, *Lawrence Collection, L_ROY_09178*; pages 50–51, *A.H. Poole Collection, P_WP_0690*; page 52, *Lawrence Collection, L_CAB_09054*; page 53, *A.H. Poole Collection, P_WP_4436*; page 54, *A.H. Poole Collection, P_WP_1138*; page 55, *A.H. Poole Collection, P_WP_0796*; pages 56–7, *Clarke Collection, CLAR35*; pages 58–9, *Lawrence Collection, L_ROY_09985*; pages 60–61, *A.H. Poole Collection, P_WP_1174a*; page 62, *Dixon Album, Album 117 p052_1*; page 63, *Dixon Album, Album 117 p025_5*; pages 64–5, *A.H. Poole Collection, POOLEIMP 902*; page 66, *Dixon Album, Album 117 p031_4*; page 67, *Clarke Collection, CLAR51*; page 68, *Valentine Collection, VALVR62917*; page 69, *Clonbrock Collection, CLON860*; pages 70–71, *Clonbrock Collection, CLON486*; pages 72–3, *A.H. Poole Collection, P_WP_1611*; page 74, *A.H. Poole Collection, P_WP_1388*; page 75, *A.H. Poole Collection, POOLEIMP 467*; pages 76–7, *Tempest Collection, TEM_129*; pages 78–9, *A.H. Poole Collection, P_WP_1796*; pages 80–81, *A.H. Poole Collection, P_WP_2085*; pages 82–3, *A.H. Poole Collection, P_WP_2491*; page 84, *A.H. Poole Collection, POOLE_O_7639*; page 85, *Tempest Collection, TEM_043*; pages 86–7, *Congested Districts Board Collection, CDB97*; pages 88–9, *Congested Districts Board Collection, CDB96*; pages 90–91, *Eason Collection, EAS_4070*; pages 92–3, *Eason Collection, EAS_4071*; pages 94–5, *A.H. Poole Collection, P_WP_2494*; pages 96–7, *A.H. Poole Collection, P_WP_2708*; pages 98–9, *Keogh Collection, Ke 210*; pages 100–101, *W.D. Hogan Collection, HOG183*; pages 102–3, *Hogan-Wilson Collection, HOGW 90*; pages 104–5, *Fitzelle Album, Fitz_4*; pages 106–7, *Fitzelle Album, Fitz_13*; pages 108–9, *W.D. Hogan Collection, HOG11*; pages 110–11, *Independent Newspapers (Ireland) Limited, IND_H_0211*; pages 112–13, *Hogan-Wilson Collection, HOGW 24*; pages 114–15, *Hogan-Wilson Collection, HOGW 141*; pages 116–17, *Independent Newspapers (Ireland) Limited, IND_H_0314*; pages 118–19, *A.H. Poole Collection, P_WP_3171*; pages 120–21, *W.D. Hogan Collection, HOG221*; pages 122–3, *A.H. Poole Collection, P_WP_3148*; pages 124–5, *W.D. Hogan Collection, HOG184*; pages 126–7, *A.H. Poole Collection, P_WP_3515*; pages 128–9, *Independent Newspapers (Ireland) Limited, IND_H_1213*; pages 130–31, *A.H. Poole Collection, P_WP_3734*; pages 132–3, *A.H. Poole Collection, P_WP_3735*; page 134, *A.H. Poole Collection, POOLE_K_2030a-5*; page 135, *A.H. Poole Collection, P_WP_3910*; pages 136–7, *Independent Newspapers (Ireland) Limited, IND_H_1944*; pages 138–9, *Independent Newspapers (Ireland) Limited, IND_H_1900*; page 140, *A.H. Poole Collection, P_WP_4003*; page 141, *A.H. Poole Collection, P_WP_4002*; page 142, *A.H. Poole Collection, P_WP_4001*; page 143, *A.H. Poole Collection, P_WP_4000*; pages 144–5, *A.H. Poole Collection, P_WP_4102*; pages 146–7, *Independent Newspapers (Ireland) Limited, IND_H_3064*; pages 148–9, *Independent Newspapers (Ireland) Limited, IND_H_3221*; page 150, *O'Dea Album, ODEA1/89a*; page 151, *O'Dea Album, ODEA1/89b*; pages 152–3, *Independent Newspapers (Ireland) Limited, IND_H_2900*; page 154, *O'Dea Album, ODEA 1/91*; page 155, *O'Dea Album, ODEA 3/61*; pages 156–7, *Independent Newspapers (Ireland) Limited, IND_H_3339*; page 158, *Album 396*; page 159, *O'Dea Album, ODEA 2/57*; pages 160–61, *Valentine Collection, VAL 2900*; pages 162–3, *Independent Newspapers (Ireland) Limited, IND43.965*; page 164, *A.H. Poole Collection, P_WP_4402*; page 165, *Independent Newspapers (Ireland) Limited, IND6.776*; pages 166–7, *W.D. Hogan, HOG236*; pages 168–9, *A.H. Poole Collection, P_WP_4617*; pages 170–71, *Cardall Collection, CARDALL_292_9-1*; pages 172–3, *A.H. Poole Collection, P_WP_4627*; pages 174–5, *A.H. Poole Collection, P_WP_4658*; pages 176–7, *Colman Doyle, CDOY 2*; page 178, *Wiltshire Collection, WIL a7[53]*; page 179, *Colman Doyle, CDoy83*; page 180, *Wiltshire Collection, WIL 13[54]*; page 181, *Wiltshire Collection, WIL f3[54]*; pages 182–3, *Wiltshire Collection, WIL e2[54]*; page 184, *Colman Doyle, CDOY43*; page 185, *Wiltshire Collection, WIL 8[6]*; pages 186, *Wiltshire Collection, WIL 6[1]*; page 187, *Wiltshire Collection, WIL 9[5]*; page 188, *Wiltshire Collection, WIL 3[11]*; page 189, *Wiltshire Collection, WIL 2[10]*; page 190, *Wiltshire Collection, WIL 11[9]*; page 191, *Wiltshire Collection, WIL 19[7]*; page 192, *Wiltshire Collection, WIL 47[12]*; page 193, *Wiltshire Collection, WIL 44[6]*; pages 194–5, *Wiltshire Collection, WIL 45[9]*; page 196, *Wiltshire Collection, WIL 45[4]*; page 197, *Wiltshire Collection, WIL 50[7]*; page 198, *Wiltshire Collection, WIL 43[4]*; page 199, *Wiltshire Collection, WIL 56[5]*; page 200, *Independent Newspapers (Ireland) Limited, INDBF969-10[17]*; page 201, *Wiltshire Collection, WIL 47[5]*; pages 202–3, *Wiltshire Collection, WIL 43[7]*; pages 204–5, *Galbraith Collection, GALBRAITH_6_31*; pages 206–7, *Galbraith Collection, GALBRAITH_12_10a*; pages 208–9, *Galbraith Collection, Galbraith_1_20a*

Bibliography/Suggested Further Reading

Bell, Jonathan and Mervyn Watson, *A History of Irish Farming 1750–1950*, Four Courts Press, 2009

Brady, Joseph and Angret Simms (eds), *Dublin Through Space and Time*, Four Courts Press, 2001

Central Council of Na Fianna Éireann, *Fianna Handbook — Irish National Boy Scouts*, 1914

Cunningham, Hugh, *The Invention of Childhood*, BBC Books, 2006

Gernsheim, Alison, *Victorian and Edwardian Fashion, A Photographic Survey*, Dover Publications Inc., 1963, 1981

Jeffrey, Ian, *Photography, A Concise History*, Thames & Hudson World of Art, 1981

Kelly, Liam, *Photographs and Photography in Irish Local History*, Maynooth Research Guides Irish Local History, 2008

Marshall, Noreen, *Dictionary of Children's Clothes*, V&A Publishing, 2008

National Archives of Ireland, Census Online, *http://www.census.nationalarchives.ie/*

Pols, Robert, *Family Photographs 1860–1945*, Public Record Office, Genealogist's Guides, 2002

Rose, Clare, *Children's Clothes Since 1750*, B.T. Batsford Limited, 1989

Rouse, Sarah, *Into the Light: An Illustrated Guide to the Photographic Collections of the National Library of Ireland*, National Library of Ireland, 1998

Shrimpton, Jayne, *Family Photographs & How to Date Them*, Countryside Books, 2008

Shrimpton, Jayne, *How to the get most from Family Pictures*, Society of Genealogists Enterprises Ltd, 2011

Tuke, James Hack, *Irish distress and its remedies: the land question; A visit to Donegal and Connaught in the spring of 1880*, W. Ridgeway, 1880

Unknown, *Simple Lessons in Physical Drill*, Blackie & Son, 1909